ROMAN CHESTER
'DEVA

TEXT, GRAPHICS AND PUBLICATION BY
GORDON EMEI
27 GLADSTONE ROAD, CHESTER CH1 4BZ
www.gordonemery.co.uk

INCLUDING
'GRAHAM WEBSTER GALLERY OF ROMAN STONES'
BY
ROY WILDING ©2003

*Antefix (roof end tile) with a boar symbol of the XX Legion 'Valeria Victrix'
deployed at DEVA from about 86 AD to 287 AD, made in the clay fields of Holt, upriver.*

CONTENTS

Cover: The sun sets on the Roman Empire – Deva in the third century AD/CE
© *Julian Baum   www.take27.co.uk*

ROMANS IN BRITAIN

'The Roman Imperial Army was one of the most formidable fighting machines the world has ever seen; superb in its equipment, training and discipline, it was imbued with the deep Roman sense of the fulfilment of destiny in accordance with the designs of the gods. It was composed of the legions, heavily armoured infantry, all Roman citizens and some 5,000 strong, and auxiliary units, 500 strong (from the second century AD some were 1,000) trained and equipped as cavalry, infantry and mixed units.

'There were also fleets for coastal and river patrols and transporting men and supplies. All this required a vast supporting organisation for supplies, armaments, communications, transport, recruitment and training. The legions were the main fighting force of the first and second centuries and also became the builders and engineers responsible for the forts and the frontier works like Hadrian's Wall.'

Graham Webster 'Roman Britain'

Celtic tribes ruled Britain in the Iron Age, often making defences at hill-forts, keeping animals on farmsteads in the cleared forests, and sometimes growing crops. Julius Caesar, who claimed that *'the people... do not grow corn but live on milk and meat and dress in skins',* carried out an almost abortive invasion of southern England in BC54 resulting in some tributes from southeastern tribes and exports of corn, cattle, gold, silver, iron, slaves and hounds – but, with changes in leaders, the tributes stopped.

In 40AD Caligula assembled the legions in Gaul (France), apparently for invasion then told his soldiers to collect seashells.

The Romans finally invaded Britannia in AD43 under Claudius. By 60 AD Wales was conquered under Nero – the mighty legions fought the fierce Ordovician tribe of western Albion. To attack the Island of Mona (Anglesey) the soldiers built flat boats to cross the strait. The cavalry rode or swam with their horses. On reaching the far bank they found, interspersed with the men, women dressed in black *'like furies'* holding torches, and the druids chanting and cursing. The soldiers were stunned but were urged forward by their commander and slaughtered the barbarians. Suetonius Paullinus then returned east and south with the XIV and part of the XX legions to re-establish control in the southern kingdoms where the warrior Queen Boudicca of the Iceni, after being abused by the Romans, had rebelled, rampaged, killed and destroyed. Short of supplies and outnumbered by at least eight to one, Paullinus decided to fight anyway. At the final battle the British army was massacred, the losers getting trapped by their own wagons at the edge of the battle site.

The rebuilding of Londinium soon began. The II Legion "Adiutrix Pia Fidelis ' (helper, pious and faithful – to Vespasian) marched northwest and built the fort at Chester (DEVA), before being posted to the Rhine probably around 86AD. Chester eventually became the headquarters of the XX Legion 'Valeria' who had vanquished Boudicca and earned the additional title 'Victrix', a name later added to the fortress.

The army now turned their attention to the Brigantian lands in northern England, and the Votadini, Selgovae, Novantae and Damnonii of southern Scotland. Under Governor Agricola the XX Legion progressed northwards through Lancaster and established forts up the northwest coast including Carlisle (LUGUVALIUM) built as early as AD72. The IX Legion 'Hispana' probably advanced north from York (EBORICUM).

Agricola's army in Scotland (CALEDONIA) probably had 30,000 men including the IX Legion from York and the XX from Wroxeter as well as auxiliaries, fighting a battle near Inverness in AD84 and killing some 10,000 Caledonians with only 360 losses. However by 100AD Scotland had been abandoned with large losses recorded. The legionary fortresses at Chester and York were rebuilt in stone. Rome was reaching the peak of its Empire.

It is around this time that the IX Legion disappears from records in one of the greatest mysteries of Roman rule in Britain. Many theories have been expounded: that they were dissolved, destroyed or sent to Europe (officers of the Legion have been recorded in the Netherlands, but these may have just been from an attachment). The last record of the IX Legion in Britain is at York in c107AD. The possible loss in battle of the IX in Scotland has resulted in a number of fictional books such as 'Eagle of the Ninth' also made into a TV series and film.

The defining point of consolidation between Scotland and England was the visit in 122AD by Hadrian, who probably brought the VI Legion 'Victrix' with him, presumably to make up for the lost or transferred IX Legion. He had decided to build a defensive wall from the east coast to the west coast, resulting in 73 miles of stone wall (80 Roman miles) and turf wall with 16 supporting forts interspersed with milecastles. An astounding 27 million cubic feet of stone were used in the wall's construction and 10,000 men garrisoned for its defence.

Coin of the Emperor Hadrian (117-138)

Although 'Hadrian's Wall' was immediately abandoned after his death, by Emperor Antoninus Pius, to build the more northerly 'Antonine Wall' - a turf wall and ditch - it was later refortified by Emperor Marcus Aurelius in c164AD. The Roman Empire had now over-extended. Although Emperor Septimus Severus reconquered Scotland to the Antonine Wall the Romans withdrew once more to Hadrian's Wall after the Brigantian uprising at the turn of the third century. The Roman Empire was now in decline but the Wall was held for another two centuries until the legions left Britain to defend itself.

An amazing record of daily life, probably representative of all British forts, has been built of life on the Wall after the discovery, at Vindolanda fort in Northumbria, of handwritten material on wooden tablets including lists of supplies, men, and letters (the Roman equivalent of postcards) between forts. Inked letters are in Roman cursive script. *See: vindolanda.csad.ox.ac.uk*

As an example, a strength report from the First Cohort of Tungrians shows, out of 752 men, 337 men were at Coria, 46 were guards of the governor, others elsewhere were listed, leaving 296 of which 15 were sick, 6 were wounded and 10 suffering eye inflammation.

Food supplies were common letters or lists, while personal letters included one officer's wife, one of the few women allowed in a fort, inviting another to a birthday celebration. There were applications for leave, official letters, travelling expenses, orders for food and clothing, orders for cart parts, loans and bills. Names include Celtic, German, Spanish and Greek; officers mentioned including a consul, a legate, at least 16 centurions, with decurions and optiones. In one mention of the locals they were sarcastically called '*Brittunculi*' the Latin equivalent of 'little Britons'.

ROMAN FORTRESS DEVA

A small primary Roman fort may have existed at Chester as early as 60 AD. However the main fortress was built in about 75 AD by the Roman II Legion on a rocky sandstone outcrop at the mouth of the sacred Celtic river, Dyfrdwy in the former territory of the Cornovii opposite that of the Deceangli. The legion appeased the holy waters by naming their turf and wooden fortress DEVA. Free from the floods of winter and ever-changing shorelines of the estuary, the site was ideal as a western port to import supplies, export lead and slaves, and attack the north and *Ierne* (Ireland).

galea (helmet)

pilum (javelin)

lorica segmenta (shoulder armour)

gladius (short sword)

tunica di lana (woollen tunic)

balteus (belt)

cingulum (groin protection)

pugio (dagger) [not visible]

scutum (embossed shield)

caligae (sandals)

A Roman legionary

After the XX Legion took over the fortress in around 90 AD, they began to rebuild it in stone around 102 AD.

Centurial Stone: '(Built by) the century of Ocratius Maximus, in the first cohort' LMP may be reference to a thousand units of distance or the initials of the stonemason.

However, only twenty years later, the legion marched north to build the momentous wall for Emperor Hadrianus, leaving the fort as a supply and administrative garrison, ideal for sending supplies up the west coast.

By 163AD wall building in Scotland was abandoned: the XX Legion returned to reoccupy and rebuild DEVA around 200AD. In the fourth century, the army used old gravestones in its reconstruction of the north wall.

Outside the walls a *canabae* (civilian settlement) developed to supply labour, goods and women for the vast force of soldiers assembled here from all over the Continent. Outside the walls, also, cemeteries lined the Roman roads with highly coloured carvings and inscriptions. Temples to the gods were set up to ensure the soldiers', and the priests', good fortune.

A *praetorium* (palace) for the legate stood opposite the huge columns of the *principia* of the legionary headquarters. Inside were kept the standards of the legion, and beneath, in the strongroom at the heart of the fortress, the wages of the soldiers.

The enormous fort, the largest in Britain, also contained a unique oval building, perhaps intended to become a governor's residence or the seat of government, however it was abandoned when the troops went north to build Hadrian's Wall and only completed in the third century.

Barracks lined the north and south walls. Granaries and stores were kept within the fortifications. Both inside and outside the walls were bath-houses *thermae*. Here the men could think of warmer climes as they relaxed and chatted to their friends about the sport in the amphitheatre and news of the empire.

Greek doctors employed in the fort practised their life-supporting arts and erected altars to *Aesclepius* of the gentle hands, *Hygeia* and *Panakeia*. Aesclepius was the Greek god of healing and medicine, Hygeia, his daughter, goddess of health, and Panacea, another daughter was another goddess of health able to 'heal-all'. Doctors here were treated as officers without fatigues.

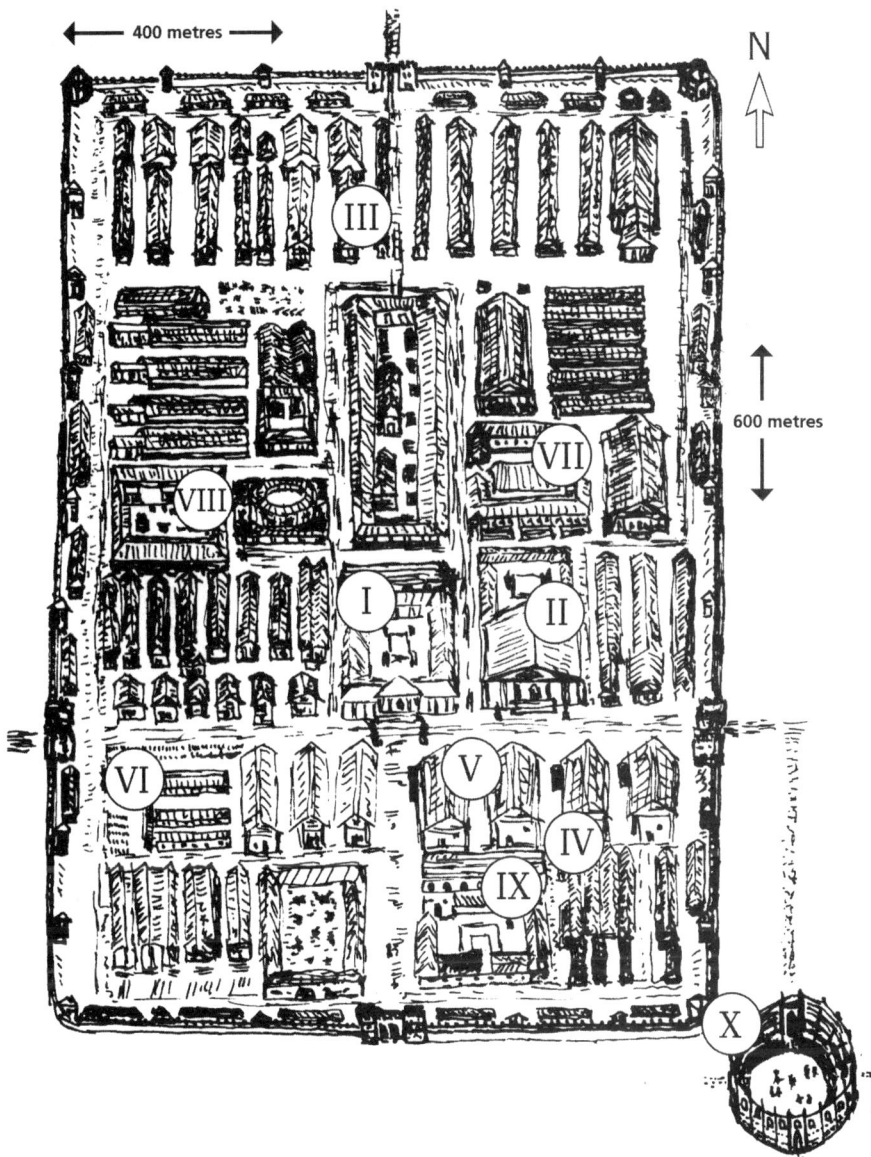

Plan of DEVA

I *Principia* (HQ)   II *Praetorium* (Legate's Palace)
III *Centuriae* (Legionary barracks)   IV *Auxilia* (Auxiliary barracks)
V *Scamnum Tribonorum*   (Tribunes' houses)   VI *Horrea* (Granaries) VII
Valetudinaria (Hospital buildings)   VIII *Fabrica* (Workshops)
IX *Thermae* (Baths)   X *Circus* (Amphitheatre)

However, it was the Roman gods and goddesses who received the most favour. Altars and shrines to Jupiter, Fortuna, Minerva, and gods of the household and legion stood in the buildings. A princeps of the legion erected a shrine to Jupiter.

On the rebuilding of the amphitheatre or perhaps later, the centurion Sextus Marcianus, after a vision, had an altar to Nemesis, set up by the north door. During the execution of criminals this would serve to remind soldiers and citizens that the law of Rome, carried out by men, was based on divine rulings. Afterwards Nemesis would transport the souls of the guilty to Tartarus: the abyss of punishment below Hades where the Titans were confined.

Altar to Nemesis, set up 'after a vision' by Sextus Marcianus

In the enormous amphitheatre crowds flocked in and took their seats around the 40 feet / 11.5 metre high oval. Some may have reserved regular seats – on top of the arena wall Seranus had his name inscribed *Seranus locus* (Seranus' place).

The excitement built up over the day. Through the north entrance the morning's parade, music, a sacrifice, mock fights, executions of criminals, and animal fights leading up to the main events in the afternoon. With take-away snacks in thin pottery cups decorated with gladiatorial scenes, the soldiers would be eating, drinking and betting on their favourite gladiator, some who fought only a few times a year and often survived as heroes. Others who had lost but fought well would also be spared to fight again, the crowd signalling for their fate: death or deliverance.

Death in the amphitheatre

The boar, symbol of the XX Legion, faced the tiled roofs on antefixes. Many were left or buried when the legions departed to Gaul (France) along with hoards of silver and other riches too dangerous or heavy to carry, some not discovered to this day. A garrison appears to have held Chester until the 390s.

When the Saxons found the city they attributed the buildings to a race of giants. Ranulph Higden, a 14th century monk saw *great stones inscribed with the names of the ancients, pillars and double vaults of stone.* Much of this stone would have been reused in church buildings such as the former minster and cathedral church of St John the Baptist.

The amphitheatre, robbed of surface stone, lay hidden until its discovery in the 1930s when the new inner ring-road had to be diverted around it, and it was finally excavated thanks to the perseverance of the Chester Archaeological Society.

ROMAN REMAINS IN CHESTER

A mythical beast with a scarlet eye in a green enamel body is an example of Romano-British art on a seal box lid dug up under the Storyhouse in Northgate Street.

Street patterns. Look up at the street names by The Cross to see the former Roman names of the streets, two feet underneath.

At Edgar's Field in Handbridge near the Roman crossing point of the Dee stands a **shrine to Minerva** with her owl, the only in situ Roman stone shrine in Britain.

Minerva shrine

She was patron of all the rivers and springs in Britania. In Bath she had been linked with the Celtic goddess Sulis. She was fast becoming the most popular deity representing soldiers, crafts and wisdom. Also known as Pallas and Athena she was worshipped in the five day March festival of Quinquatrix in Rome, where oblations, gladatorial contests and a parade took place. The cave beside her statue may have been used by a Mithraic cult, with its baptisms and sacraments of wine and bread, that appealed to soldiers in the far-flung borders of the empire. Constantine suppressed the cult when he became a Christian. The shrine appears to have survived because it was once believed to have been a carving of the the Virgin Mary.

A **bronze discharge certificate** (copy) at the Grosvenor Museum dating to 103 AD was found in nearby Malpas. The retired cavalry troop leader from Spain had led a group who nowadays would be called Hungarians. Reading the discharge certificate, one wonders whether he had one wife or had to choose.

Translation of discharge certificate:
Emperor Caesar Nerva Trajan Augustus, conqueror of Germany and Dacia, son of the deified Nerva, Great Priest, in the seventh year of his Tribunician power, four times saluted Imperator, Father of his country, five times Consul, to the cavalry and infantry who are serving in the four squadrons and eleven cohorts named: First Thracians (Turkey), First Pannonian Tampiana (Hungary), Sebosius' Gauls (France), Vettonian Spaniards Roman Citizens (Spain), First Spanish (Spain), Vengiones 1,000 strong ((Bavaria), First Alpines (Switzerland), First Morinarians (Belgium), First Cogernorians (Rhine), First Bactasorians (Rhine Estuary), First Tungorians 1,000 strong (Belgium), Second Thracians (Turkey), Third Bracari (NW Spain), Third Lingones (Germany), Fourth Damations (Yugoslavia) who are in Britain under Lucius Neratius Marcellus, and have served for 25 or more years each and where names are appended, has granted citizenship for them, their children and heirs, together with the right of legal marriage with the wives they had when citizenship was granted, or, if they are unmarried those they have subsequently married as long as it is only one.
January 19th, in the second consulship of Manius Laberius Maximus and Quintus Glitius Atilius Agricola.
For the Decurion Reburrus, son of Severus, from Spain, in the First Squadron Pannonian Tampians commanded by Gaius Valerius Celsus.
Copied from and compared with the bronze tablet affixed in Rome to the wall behind the temple of the deified Augustus near [the statue of] Minerva.
[Witnessed by] Quintus Pompeius Homerus, Gaius Pabius Esubes,Titus Flavius Secundus, Publius Caulus Vitalis, Gaius Vettiennus Modestus, Publius Atinius Hedonicus, Tiberius Claudius Menander.

During 1821, in the cellar of 39 Bridge Street (Spud-U-Like) 33 stone pillars of a *hypocaust* from a *thermae* (bathhouse) were found. Each was 84cm high, supporting large square perforated tiles which heated the *sudatarium* (sweating room). The cellar is open to the public.

Another **hypocaust** can be seen in 12 Northgate Street (when the shop is occupied) by asking the shop staff.

Pieces from another moved **hypocaust** are in the Roman Gardens by the Newgate off Pepper Street, along with **Roman columns** from the baths and stone fragments.

It was in the baths that the soldiers could relax, chat to their friends, warm up and 'chill out' literally with the *sudatarium* (steam rooms), *calidarium* (hot plunge bath) and *frigidarium (*cold plunge bath). Baths were also built outside the fortress, encouraging local citizens to take up the Roman way of life.

A **Roman Angle Tower** base can be seen beside the Newgate. Originally inside the fortress walls it is now on the outside due to the fallen wall being rebuilt further back.

Part of the **Roman Eastgate** in the shape of an arch survives on the north side (over Dinky Donuts).

The **Grosvenor Museum** (free entry) holds the **best preserved Roman gravestones in northwest Europe** in its Graham Webster Gallery of Roman Stones (see next chapter). Roman artefacts from the city can also be seen including a **lead ingot** from 74AD found in the mud of the Roman port, dropped perhaps by some careless dockhand, and **lead water pipes** of 79AD inscribed with Governor Agricola's name.   *01244 972197*

Lead ingot

Gladiator tile depicting a retiarius (net man)

The enormous stone **amphitheatre**, the largest military one in Britain, could hold 8,000 spectators. It has been partially excavated and can be found next to the Newgate. A **tile** found nearby shows a retiarius (gladiator with trident and net).

Roman column bases from the *principia*, still in situ can be seen in the cellar of 23 Northgate Row West (Pret a manger).

The **Roman strongroom,** at the heart of the fort, within the *principia* can be seen adjacent to the Dublin Packet pub on Northgate Street. Here the fort kept its money and the savings of the soldiers after taking their living expenses. The soldiers staple diet was wheat harvested from the Cheshire plains.

Look up from the Northgate Canal Bridge back towards the shops on the wall. Here is the best preserved section of **Roman Wall -** thirteen courses without mortar, now slightly bulging.

More of the Roman Wall can be seen along the east wall base from the car park in the former abbey kaleyards also known as the Hop Pole Paddock.

A repositioned **cornice** (two coping stones) can be seen in the small park off Water Tower Street by the Northgate.

Section of repositioned coping stones in the park beside Water Tower Street

The **Dewa Roman Experience** just west of Bridge Street takes visitors via the dark hold of a Roman galley* to the sights, smells and sounds of DEVA including barracks, market stalls and taverna. (The different spelling of the fortress name is based on the suggestion that 'v' was pronounced as a softer 'w'). Complete with an open archaeological dig, Roman artefacts and Roman tours, there is a charge for entry.   ***01244 343407***

* an idea by the author of this guide

GRAHAM WEBSTER GALLERY OF ROMAN STONES

'Epigraphy the study of inscriptions:
One of the most important aspects of this period
(the Roman occupation of Britain)
is the sudden introduction of literacy
and the habit of the Romans to carve inscriptions
on stone and metal recording their names
and other actions of a public and private nature.
There are thus hundreds of commemorative stones, tombstones,
Altars, proprietary marks... It is from this vast body of information
that we can piece together the history of the Province...'

Graham Webster 'Roman Britain'

Victorian Revelations

In 1883 repairs were being carried out to a length of the city wall near to the tower known as Morgan's Mount, about halfway between the Northgate and the Water Tower. I.Matthews Jones, the City Surveyor, noticed that the interior of the lower courses of the wall contained fragments of Roman stonework, including part of a tombstone.

More extensive repairs to the walls took place in 1887, on a stretch between the Northgate and King Charles Tower. This time, so many Roman stones were discovered that the work was extended, and even more were found. Like the stones recovered in 1883, they were all buried within the interior of the lower part of the wall. The sculptures and inscriptions on the stones made it clear that they had come from Roman cemeteries.

In addition to the inscribed stones there were also a number of sculpted panels. These had once decorated large tombs or funeral monuments. Since Roman law forbade the burial of the dead within a built-up area, the cemetery or cemeteries must have lain outside the fortress walls.

Overjoyed by these magnificent finds, the Chester Archaeological Society and other interested groups pooled their resources to examine the stretch of wall west of the Northgate. Between 1890 and 1892 more collections of inscriptions, tombstones and sculptures were recovered. Altogether, between 1883 and 1892, over 150 stones were found.

Although a few Roman stones had been found in Chester before this date and a number have been found since, the discoveries in the north wall in those nine years still remain one of the most spectacular archaeological finds in Britain. Many of these stones are now superbly displayed in the award winning Graham Webster Gallery.

There is no great mystery how and why these artefacts had been hidden for so long in the walls. Although law prohibited private individuals from disturbing graves in Roman times, it seems to have been common practice to use gravestones to reinforce defences:

'Several towns in Gaul drew on their cemeteries when they set up defensive walls in the late third century, notably at Strasbourg and Neumagen; in Britain, Lincoln and London provide striking examples of this usage...'

R P Wright & I A Richmond 'The Roman Inscribed and Sculptured Stones in the Grosvenor Museum' Chester 1955

A World of Colour

Today's stones don't do justice to the colour and excitement of the Roman world. A world of toil for soldiers was offset by the luxury and thrills of leisure time. Inside the fort strict army rule was enforced but outside were the temples, the amphitheatre, the traders, the whorehouses, and hundreds of brightly painted funeral stones depicting, on many, the richness of the deceased's earthly life or the glory of an expected afterlife.

Amazingly some of the sandstone used for the monuments did not come from the bedrock of Chester but from better quality sandstone beds eight miles away.

Into the Darkness

When Romans were at the point of death, their nearest relative present endeavoured to catch the last breath with their mouth. The ring was taken off the finger of the dying person. As soon as they were dead, the nearest relation closed the eyes and mouth of the dead body.

Then they called on the deceased by name, exclaiming,*'have'* or *'vale'*. The corpse was then washed, and anointed with oil and perfumes by slaves who belonged to the undertakers. A small coin was then placed in the mouth of the corpse, in order to pay the ferryman in Hades. The corpse was laid out on a couch in the vestibule of the house, with its feet towards the door. It was dressed in the best robe that the deceased had worn alive. Ordinary citizens were dressed in a white toga while magistrates wore their official robes.

If the deceased had received a crown for their bravery, it was now placed on their head. The couch on which they were laid was sometimes covered with leaves and flowers. A branch of cypress was also usually placed at the door of the house if the deceased was a person of consequence.

Funerals were usually *exsequiae* or *funera justa;* the former term was generally appiled to the funeral procession *(pompa funebris).* There were two kinds of funerals, public and private: the public one was a *funus publicum,* where a herald invited the people to it. The private funeral was a *funus tacitum, translatitium,* or *plebeium.*

A person usually left a certain sum of money in their will to pay the expenses of the funeral; but if they did not, nor appoint anyone to bury them, this duty devolved upon the persons to whom the deceased's property was left. If they died without a will, then the responsibility for the funeral fell upon their relations according to their order of succession to the deceased's property. The expenses of the funeral, were in such cases, decided by an arbiter according to the property and rank of the deceased; *arbitia* is used to signify the funeral expenses.

When wealthy Romans died, funerals were conducted with great pomp and ceremony, which was, of course, not the case for persons in ordinary circumstances. In the early days of Rome, all funerals were performed at night. However, later on, rich people held elaborate funerals during daylight hours, so that they could show off their wealth. The poor were only buried at night because they could not afford a funeral procession.

Bring on the Clowns

The corpse was carried out of the house on the eighth day after death. A person called a *Designator* or *Dominus Funeris* regulated the order of the funeral procession, and was attended by *lictors* dressed in black. Heading the procession were musicians who played mournful music. Next came mourning women, *Praeficae,* who were hired to lament and sing the funeral song in praise of the deceased. Players and buffoons sometimes followed these. One, called *Archimimus*, represented the character of the deceased and imitated his words and actions. Then came the slaves who the deceased had liberated, wearing the *pileati,* cap of liberty; occasionally there were many, since the master sometimes liberated all his slaves in his will, in order to add to the pomp at his funeral.

Before the corpse, people often walked wearing waxen masks representing the ancestors of the deceased, and were clothed in the official dress of whom they represented; there were also carried before the corpse the crowns or military awards which the deceased had gained.

The corpse was carried on a *lectica* (couch), to which the name of *freretum* or c*apulus* was given; but the bodies of poor citizens and slaves were carried on a common kind of bier or coffin, a s*andapila.* This was carried by bearers, *vespae* or *vespillones,* because they carried the corpses in the evening. The couches on which the corpses of the rich were carried were sometimes made of ivory, and covered with gold and purple. They were often carried on the shoulders of the nearest relation of the deceased, and sometimes by the freedmen.

The relations of the deceased walked behind the corpse in mourning; sons with their heads veiled, and daughters with their heads bare and their hair dishevelled, contrary to the usual practice of both. They often uttered loud lamentations, and the women beat their breasts and tore their cheeks, though law forbade this. The corpse was carried to the place of burning or burial, which, according to law was obliged to be outside the city.

After the dead person had been put to rest at the funeral, the friends returned home. They then underwent *suffitio (*purification), which consisted of being sprinkled with water and stepping over a fire. There were also other acts of purification called *exverrae* using a certain kind of broom. The mourning and solemnities with the dead lasted for nine days after the funeral. At the end a sacrifice, *Novendiale*, was performed.

Gone but not Forgotten

The Romans, like the Greeks, were accustomed to visit the tombs of their relatives at certain periods, and to offer them sacrifices and various gifts, called *inferiae* and *parentalia*. The Romans appear to have regarded the *manes* or departed souls of their ancestors as gods; hence arose the practice of presenting to them oblations, which consisted of wine, milk, garlands of flowers, and other things. The tombs were sometimes illuminated with lamps on these occasions.

In the latter end of February there was a festival, *Feralia,* in which the Romans were accustomed to carry food to the sepulchres for the use of the dead. The Romans, like ourselves, were accustomed to wearing mourning for their deceased friends, which appears to have been black or dark blue, under the Republic, for both sexes. Under the Empire the men continued to wear black in mourning, but the women wore white. They laid aside all kinds of ornaments, and did not cut either their hair or beard. Men appear to have usually worn their mourning clothes for only a few days, but women for a year when they lost a husband or parent.

Beyond the Veil

The sepulchral banquet type of relief was first found in pre-Roman, Assyrian, Etruscan, Greek monuments, and around forts on the Rhine frontier. The reclining figure of the departed is celebrating their own life and death, and the passing of the soul to the Blessed Isles. It is as if the deceased (represented on the stone) is present with the mourners at their own wake, proposing a toast in a *poculum* or cup. The tripod table (or three-legged stool) is full of rich offerings. No evidence of the significance, if any, of the three-legged stool's constant presence on sepulchral banquet stones can be found. It may be just to its everyday use in Roman life. However three supporting legs do sometimes represent stability.

Described hereafter are the majority of stones on display in the Graham Webster Gallery at the Grosvenor Museum. The museum's numbering has been retained while the number in brackets comes from the main reference source: *The Roman Inscribed and Sculptured Stones in the Grosvenor Museum, Chester* 1955 by R P Wright & I A Richmond. This uses the same numbering system as the Catalogue of 1900.

Stone no.21 (108)

To the memory of the departed, Curalia Dinysia aged 40 years; erected by her heir.

This stone shows the dead lady enjoying a banquet. She reclines on a couch. In her hand Curatia holds a drinking cup. A tripod stands in front of the couch. Above the stone are two birds perched on garlands of leaves. Birds were thought to bring good fortune and to represent the soul's freedom to escape after death. At the top corners are tritons, half-men, half-fish, blowing on seashell horns. This connection with the sea reflects the belief that the souls of the dead travelled across the ocean to a happier life in the Isles of the Blessed.

Stone no.20 (115)

To the departed spirits of Flavius Callimorphus, aged 42, and Seraphon, aged 3 years and 6 months. Thesaeus set this up to brother and son.

On this tombstone a gabled niche contains a funeral couch with baluster legs, mattress, cushion and high ends, upon which reclines Callimorphus with Serapion held close. The legs of the couch rest upon high blocks, between which stands to the right a three-legged dining table, on which perches a tiny bird, and to the left a carrot-shaped wine jar. It was found in 1874 with two skeletons, a gold ring, and a 'second bronze' coin of Domitian, while making a sewer along the west Walls, about 12 metres from the Walls and not far from the junction with Grosvenor Road, that is southwest of the Roman fortress. It is not clear whether the boy was the son of Callimorphus or Thesaeus. It probably dates from the end of the first century AD. These names are Greek, they may have been freedmen or traders.

Stone no.22 (113)

*To the spirits of the departed, …
mine (bottom part of stone is missing
and only part of the inscription remains).*

In this example a large seashell canopy
has a dolphin either side. The lady who
has died reclines on her couch. She
holds a cup in her right hand. On the
other a ring adorns her little finger.
Beneath the couch is the usual three-
legged table. The seashells and dolphins
are a reference to the voyage of the
lady's soul to the Isles of the Blessed.

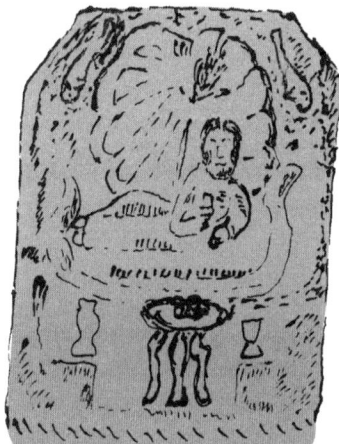

The Cavalry

*'The army was in a constant state of change to meet the new enemies and
pressures from without. In the third and fourth centuries it became far more
mobile with points of static defences held by the old traditional units, but the
brunt of the fighting was borne by the new field armies, almost entirely
mounted and heavily armoured.'*
Graham Webster 'Roman Britain'

Stone no.16 (85)

*To the spirits of the departed and
Aurelius Lucius, cavalryman.
His heir had this made.*

The exotic scene on this stone
shows the bearded man, Aurelius,
reclining on a couch. He holds up a
drinking cup in his right hand. His
short sword and helmet complete
with plume of feathers are displayed.
In front are a three-legged table, a
boy attendant or slave and a single
severed head. The man holds his
scrolled will in his left hand.

21

The Romans usually recruited their cavalry from the less civilised parts of the Empire. Aurelius' appearance with a large fearsome moustache and stiff spiky hair suggests that he came from a barbarian background. This impression is increased by the severed head, which may represent a trophy from hunting during a battle or raid.

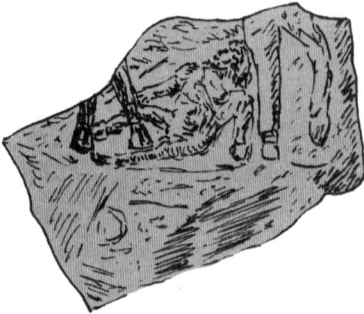

Stone no.15 (99)

To the spirits of the departed,
(rest of the inscription is missing).

A fragment which, when it was complete, commemorated a Roman cavalryman. However, it is also a propaganda message to all enemies of Rome. It is symbolic of the ascendancy of mighty Rome over all its adversaries. A wounded barbarian, the noble savage, his naked body beautifully modelled, lies under the legs of the cavalryman's horse, his spear broken and he clings to his six-sided shield. Both his sword-belt and the hilt of his sword can be seen.

Stone no.18 (137)

Inscription missing

The rider is a Sarmatian, from a nomadic people who once lived north of the River Danube in an area now known as Hungary and western Romania.

The Sarmatians were defeated in 175AD by the Roman Emperor Marcus Aurelius. The Romans then forced them to contribute Sarmatian men to their army. Some were posted to Britain, including a force that was stationed at Ribchester in Lancashire. It may be that the rider on this stone was on detachment from Ribchester when he died at Chester.

The cloaked horseman holds aloft, with both hands, a dragon-ensign or pennon of Sarmation type, while his tall conical cap (as shown on Trajan's Column) with vertical metal frame, is of Sarmatian pattern, A sword hangs at his right side, and he is probably clad in scale armour. This attire for man and beast is characteristic of Sarmation cavalry. One authority suggests that the relief may depict a cavalryman taking part in a *Ludus Troiae* (a military display manoeuvre) and be dressed in eastern fashion.

The dragon standard, for which the Sarmatians were known and feared, consisted of a bronze dragon's head with fanged jaws wide open, mounted on top of a large pole. The back of the dragon's head was also open, and onto it was fastened a long tube made out of brightly coloured fabric. The size and shape of the holes in the dragon's head were cleverly made. When the horseman rode into battle at full gallop, the wind rushed into the dragon's mouth. The force of the wind not only filled the tail out (like a windsock) but also made a terrifying sound like a shrieking banshee.

Stone no.7 (91)

Sextus Simil[...], son of Sextus, of the Fabian voting-tribe, from Brixia (now Brescia, in north Italy)

The dead man, Sextus, is shown mounted on his walking horse with a boy attendant or slave, who is leading carrying an oval shield and two javelins. He rides on a small saddle with prominent back and front, resting on a large saddlecloth. His horse has a well-groomed mane. The attitude and proportions are reminiscent of Greek models. The attendant, In Greek fashion, wears a pointed hat, but other features are somewhat defaced.

At the top of the stone is a bust of Sextus flanked by two lions' heads, open-mouthed with tongues protruding, and with the heads of rams in their paws. Lions are often shown on Roman tombs. They are symbols of the suddenness of death.

There were two kinds of horsemen in Chester. One belonged to the cavalry wing, made up of auxiliary soldiers recruited in the less prosperous and less civilised parts of the Empire. In addition there was a small number of horsemen attached to each legion to act as scouts and messengers.

Standing Figures

Stone no.30 (120)

Inscription missing

This relief was once mistaken for a bishop and female acolyte, and became notorious as the ecclesiastical stone. It is, of course, of Roman origin.

On the left stands an elegant lady clad in a full length tunic with long pointed sleeves, a stole or scarf covering her shoulders, with straight fringed hanging ends, and a jabot (ornamental fringe). In her left hand she holds a mirror, with a knobbed handle. Her head, now defaced, had a richly braided coiffure.

At her left side stands a little maidservant or slave, with long-sleeved tunic and folded arms, on which rest a toilet-box or tray, with indistinguishable objects upon it. Her little face, with small mouth, is now mutilated.

Stone no.3 (38)

To the spirits of the departed, Caecilius Avitus of Emerita (a colonia in Lusitania, now Merida in Spain), optio of the Twentieth Legion, Valeria Victrix, served 15 and lived 34 years. His heir had this erected.

This complete stone shows a bearded option, Caecillius Avitus. He was a junior officer, second in rank to a centurion. His duties included some bookkeeping for the century, so he holds his accounts. He is dressed in a *sagum* (heavy cloak); the ends cross and hang down his front in two tails. His right hand holds a tall staff. A sword with massive round pommel hangs on his right side. Below the cloak a kilt reaches to his knees. The lower parts of his legs are thick and stumpy.

Stone no.9 (37)

To the spirits of the departed, Manius Aurelius Nepos, centurion of the Twentieth Legion, Valeria Victrix, lived 50 years; his most dutiful wife had this set up.

The letter before AVR in the second line resembles the usual symbol for Manius, not Marcus. However, Manius is rare and an aristocratic *praenomen*; while Marcus Aurelius is common in all cases. So it may be supposed the mason's chisel slipped.

This tombstone is made of cream-coloured Manley sandstone. A flat top niche holds the figures of the centurion Marcus Aurelius Nepos and his wife. Nepos is bare-headed and has a clipped beard. He holds a centurion's straight staff in his right hand. No attempt has been made to distinguish his tunic or corselet, but a cloak, draped over both shoulders, is fastened on his right shoulder by a knee-fibula, while a very wide belt is fastened low by a circular clasp above a full kilt falling to the knees. His legs and, in particular, arms are attenuated.

His wife, who erected the tombstone and whose name was never added, figured on a smaller scale, stands higher in the niche, on a step level with Nepos' knees, as if in the background. Minute legs peep from below a full skirt, over which falls a draped over-skirt, which she holds up with her left hand. A distaff appears to be tucked into the waist under her left arm. Her right hand carries an indistinct object, perhaps intended for a weaving comb. Her hair is arranged in tight waves, of early third century fashion.

In a recessed panel on the left side of the stone, beneath a stonemason's set-square and hammer, is the formula: *dedicated while still under the hammer.* This formula was used extensively in Illyria, Cisalpine Gaul and Transalpine Gaul, particularly in the Rhone Valley; this is the only instance yet found (up to 1955) in Britain. It seems to mark a rite of dedication to make the tomb inviolable and place it under divine protection.

Stone no.11 (90)

To the spirits of the departed, Aerelius Diogenes, Bearer of Imperial Effigy

The tombstone of an *imaginifer,* one of the many types of standard bearer in the legion. The standard that he carried was a bust of the reigning Emperor or a member of the Imperial family. It would have been made out of silvered or gilded sheet metal. The long wooden pole with handgrips can be seen: the standard tied with a scarf-like *vitta.*

Diogenes is a Greek name, implying that he may have been from, or had some connection with the eastern half of the Empire. He wears a military tunic and a *sagus* (cloak) which falls in two points at the front.

Age of Mythology

'The Roman government was very tolerant towards natives' religions, unless, like Judaism and Druidism, they had a national aspect. As newcomers, the soldiers, traders and civil servants wished to make peace with the local gods and so accepted, added and even identified many of them with the classical deities. Thus one has altars which record vows calling on the gods for aid in personal enterprise, often bearing two or more names. The Roman god Mars was thus equated with the Celtic Cocidus; Minerva with the healing god Sul at Bath.

'All natural things like rivers, springs and hills had their own gods and there were spirits that looked after every human activity in addition to the greater gods of battle, trade and crafts, health and so on. There were many shrines and temples where one could seek help and advice from the particular god or spirit and nothing was done without this essential step.

'Religion, which gave deep personal feelings or sense of brotherhood, came from the East and principal among them were Mithraism and Christianity, which were great rivals in the third century AD. The former consisted of small groups of soldiers and traders banded together for protection and assistance (somewhat akin to modern freemasonry). They worshipped in underground vaulted chambers resembling the cave in which Mithras was born. The rituals were highly secret and little is known about them, but there were seven grades of initiates who underwent trials and ordeals to prove their faith.

'Christianity became supreme because it included women and had an organisation which appealed to the Emperor Constantine,* but he hedged his bets by still allying himself to the invincible Sun god, on all his coins and inscriptions. The idea of the host of invisible spirits helping or hindering us has survived even today as superstition'

Graham Webster 'Roman Britain'

*Constantine's wife is said to have miraculously discovered the true cross of Christ (see 'Medieval Imagination in Chester Cathedrals').

Not on display (169)

No inscription

In 1853, a complete stone was found built into the wall of a cellar in Whitefriars; it shows a cross-legged youth, dressed in cloak, tunic and Phrygian cap. (Phrygia was an area in what is now Turkey.) In his right hand he holds a reversed torch.

This is *Cautopates,* one of the two attendant deities of Mithras. His occurrence implies the existence at Chester, of a *Mithraeum.*

Stone no.27

No inscription

The headless figure of a cross-legged youth with hands spread out as if in worship. He was probably the companion of one of the eastern gods, such as Mithras or Attis. The attitude of the figure would fit *Cautes,* the fellow deity of *Cautopates,* but lack of detail precludes certainty.

The stone was found in 1891 in the north wall, and was originally freestanding.

However, the two figures on the stones do not match, which may imply, if the first figure is Cautopates and the second Cautes, more than one *Mithraeum* at Chester.

Stone no.25 (170)

No inscription

A standing figure of the youthful god Attis. He was the consort of Cybele, the mother goddess, whose worship spread from the Middle East throughout the Roman Empire. The cult had mysterious rites that promised life after death. Atti's death was mourned for two days in the spring, and his recovery (when his spirit passed into a pine tree, and violets sprang up from his blood) then celebrated. Most Romans shied away from the extreme rituals such as self-castration.

On this stone he wears a tunic, cloak and Phrygian cap. He is shown as a shepherd carrying a crook. The figure faces slightly toward the left as if one member of an opposed pair, flanking a tomb.

Stone no.29 (168)

A coping stone from the surround of a funeral monument found in 1848 in Handbridge among sepulchral remains near the Roman road.

A freestanding lion, the symbol of all devouring death, crouching over its prey, apparently a stag.

Stone no.26

A sculpture showing a nude curly-headed youth with a cloak over his right shoulder. He lies dying in the shade of a carob tree, the type of tree indicating that the scene is set somewhere in the Middle East. The stone probably represents the death of Adonis, who was the favourite of the Roman goddess Venus, also identified with the Greek goddess Aphrodite, goddess of love (her cult was of Eastern origin, and she was identified with Asharte, Ishtar etc.).

The legend then goes that Adonis was killed by a boar, but was restored to life by Persephone; Zeus decreed that Adonis would spend part of each year with her and the rest on earth with Aphrodite. The use of the myth reflects the hope that the deceased will enjoy a new life beyond the grave.

Stone no.24 (141)

No inscription

A relief of a harpy, a mythical woman-headed bird, which was figurative of death or its messenger. According to a legend told by homer, Zeus blinded an evil king because of the king's cruelty. Zeus then gave orders that whenever a meal was placed before the king, the harpies should swoop down and foul the food so it was unfit for the king to eat.

Stone no.31 (172)

No inscription

A statuette of a goddess or genius (guardian spirit) seated in a stone recess. She wears a crown, holds a dish in her right hand and a large cornucopia (horn of plenty) in her left.

The statuette may have come from a shrine.

Stones no.33 (138)

No inscription

Left: Hesione, naked and bound, stands on a rock to the left. Her head is defaced. Hercules (Greek and Roman hero of prodigious strength, who performed twelve immense tasks or labours imposed on him by Eurystheus, and after death was ranked among the gods), bearded and wearing only a cloak over his left fore-arm, brandishes his club in his right hand. He advances to attack the monster, which occupied the missing right third of the scene. The subject is an allegory of salvation. **Right:** An 'anguipes' or serpent-footed monster, figurative of evil. This is not, as once suggested, the monster attacking Hesione, but a figure from a different scene on the adjoining face of the tomb.

Stone no.34 (139)

No inscription

In Greek mythology, Acteon was a hunter who, because he surprised the goddess Artemis (Diana) bathing naked with her nymphs, was changed into a stag and ripped to death by his own hounds.

Another story claims it was because Acteon boasted of his superiority in the chase. Artemis was the virgin goddess of chastity and hunting; daughter of Leto, twin sister of Apollo.

On this stone, the nude Acteon tries in vain to ward off the savaging hound on his left, and the damaged stone preserves a suggestion of another hound attacking from his right. He is already part stag, his bearded head sprouting antlers.

Altar to Nymphs

Nymphis et Fontibus

The soldiers of the XX Legion believed in the gods and the supernatural. So they took care to erect an altar beside the aqueduct which they constructed to carry water from the spring at Boughton, a mile away, to the fortress that they were building at Deva.

This they dedicated to *Nymphis et Fontibus* (nymphs and springs).

Printed by Catford Print Centre, London SE6 2PN   www.catfordprint.co.uk